Oxford International Lower Secondary

English
Workbook

9

T0346906

Eve Sullivan
Patricia Mertin
Mark Saunders

OXFORD

1 Friendship

In this unit, you will revise the first conditional, prepositions, *-ing* words and participles, the comparative and superlative forms, compound and complex sentences, and suffixes. You will write about the value of friendships, come up with some examples of anaphora and write dialogue.

The first conditional

We use conditionals to say that one thing depends on something else. The first conditional is used to talk about future situations that are real or possible.

The basic pattern is:

'If'/'Unless'/'When'/'As soon as' + present simple + 'will'/'won't' + infinitive verb

'If our friend asks for help, we will value the friendship more highly.'

The clauses can also appear the other way round:

'The acquaintanceship will not develop unless there is reciprocity.'

- Complete the sentences below.

> If I finish my assignment, *I'll come to the party.* _____
>
> As soon as it stops raining, _____
>
> They won't catch the train, _____
>
> If it's sunny tomorrow, _____
>
> You'll be cold outside today, _____

Preposition revision

- Fill in the missing prepositions.

> Friends are people who regularly cross our paths. But why do we become friends _____ with _____ one particular classmate rather than another? The key is self-disclosure. "Can I talk _____ you for a minute?" or "May I share something _____ you?" are questions which could move an acquaintanceship _____ a friendship. You are taking the risk _____ disclosing information _____ yourself. If your acquaintance listens _____ what you have to say but does not tell you anything personal _____ return, there is no reciprocity. Good friends are always there _____ us through thick and thin.

Extension Write three sentences of your own using the first conditional.

Note-taking You will need SB p8

- Summarize, in one to two sentences each, Aristotle's theory of the three kinds of friendship. Try to think of examples of each kind, perhaps from your own life, or from books, films and television programmes. Note these down too.

Writing with conviction

You have been asked by a newspaper to write about the value of friendship.

- Write your article in the space below, using your notes from the activity about summarizing Aristotle's theory on page 3 as research to support your answer. Give examples to support your ideas.

Anaphora

Anaphora is a literary device which is often used for emphasis. It occurs when a word or phrase is repeated at the beginning of a sentence or clause several times in a row. Here are some examples:

'So many places, so little time.'

'Stay safe. Stay well. Stay happy.'

'My friends are loyal; my friends are true.'

- Now write four examples of anaphora of your own, using the following words to start your series of sentences or clauses.

Give me …

I want …

When …

My school …

Extension Use your favourite anaphora example to make a hashtag for a social media post or campaign.

Two ways to say the same thing

Look at these examples.

'After establishing a friendship through self-disclosure and reciprocity, the glue that binds it is intimacy.' (**'after' + -ing form**)

'Having established a friendship through self-disclosure and reciprocity, the glue that binds it is intimacy.' (**'having' + past participle**)

- Now rewrite each of the following sentences using the alternative form.

After reading the book, I took it back to the library.

Having read the book, I took it back to the library.

After waiting half an hour for the bus, she decided to walk home.

_____

Having eaten the meal, the family cleared the table and washed up together.

_____

Having written the letter, she took it to the post office to buy a stamp.

_____

Comparative and superlative forms

- Complete each sentence using a comparative or superlative adjective, using the words in brackets to help you.

  Note whether you have used the **comparative** or **superlative** form by writing **c** or **s** after each sentence.

A mouse is (*not as big*) _____smaller_____ than an elephant. ___c___

My sister has (*a larger number*) _____ friends than I do. _____

Who has the (*many more*) _____ friends, you or me? _____

Africa is (*big*) _____ than Europe in terms of land mass. _____

Their pumpkin was the (*weighed much more than the others*)_____. _____

His kite flew (*high*) _____ still and was just a fleck in the sky. _____

It was the (*extremely low temperature*) _____ day on record. _____

Writing to online friends

- Do some research about the best ways to be safe online and write a short guide of two to three sentences here.

Writing compound and complex sentences

The following sentences are based on the extract 'A friend from the past' on pages 14–16 of your Student Book. Look at the examples below and notice how the second example is made more interesting by combining the two sentences.

'Rosie is a Year 10 student. She feels conflicted when her childhood friend, Nona, returns to her school.'

'Rosie is a Year 10 student _who_ feels conflicted when her childhood friend, Nona, returns to her school.'

- Now combine these sentences.

Nona reaches out. She takes the comprehension sheet.

_____

Selena writes on the side of her exercise book. She nudges it over so I can see.

_____

They're standing outside their classroom. They're waiting to go in.

_____

I see Nona's face fall. It is a crumple of confusion.

_____

Extension Write some pairs of sentences, as in the activity above, and then combine each pair to make a longer, more interesting sentence.

Writing dialogue

● Write your own section of dialogue between two characters that involves them meeting for the first time and getting to know each other. The setting can be anywhere you like – a fantasy world or a real place that you know. Consider where and how your characters are meeting, and their language choices, tone and register.

The suffix *-ship*

● Fill in the missing words from the list of nouns provided. They all have in common the suffix *-ship*.

championship, companionship, dictatorship, friendship, hardship, ~~membership~~, partnership, relationship

They paid an annual _____ membership _____ for the leisure centre.

During and after the war they suffered great _____.

She had trained all year for the _____.

The school was in _____ with many community organizations.

The _____ between the two countries has improved.

This isn't a democracy, it's a _____.

My dogs provide all the _____ I need.

What do you value most in a close _____?

Extension Now write a sentence of your own for each of the listed *-ship* words.

2 Travel

In this unit, you will write a social media post, revise vocabulary, rewrite sentences, practise using semicolons and opposite forms, write descriptively, and write about a future day in your life.

Writing a social media post

- Write a social media post to share your experience of a memorable day you had on holiday or when taking a day trip. Make sure the length, tone and language you use are appropriate. You might also want to add a photo or a sketch of an image you would share in your social media post.

student A ✓
@studentA

⚙ **Following**

Just had the most amazing day …

Travel vocabulary: *Around the World in Eighty Days*

- Match the words and phrases below from the extract 'In which Phileas Fogg astounds Passepartout, his servant' (Student Book pages 23–25) with their definitions.

unaccustomed	great surprise
astonishment	leaving
preparations	a person or a book/magazine/app which gives you information about a place
set foot	not used to something
native soil	charts showing the times that trains, buses and planes leave and arrive
descended	the country a person was born in
guide	to enter or visit a place
arrival	getting ready
departure	went down
timetables	reaching your destination

Rewriting sentences

Around the World in Eighty Days was published in the nineteenth century, so the language is more formal and with longer sentences than we commonly use today.

- Rewrite the following text in today's language. Can you do it using fewer words?

Original	Your turn
Passepartout, who had studied the programme of his duties, was more than surprised to see his master guilty of the inexactness of appearing at this unaccustomed hour; for, according to the rule, he was not due in Saville Row until precisely midnight.	

Descriptive writing

In 'Finding our way through the dark' on pages 27–28 of your Student Book, the author uses very descriptive language. She describes a road as, 'The worst, rudest, dismallest, darkest road I have yet travelled on …'

- Think of a road you know well and write a paragraph to describe it in the same way the author has done by using a number of superlatives and other descriptive language.

Using semicolons

Many writers like to use semicolons as they link ideas in a useful and creative way. Here is an example:

'Oliver likes reading. Books provide useful information, as well as an escape.'

'Oliver likes reading; books provide useful information, as well as an escape.'

- Join the following sentences using a semicolon (remember, the word following a semicolon should begin with a lower-case letter unless it is a proper noun).

It was hot and sunny outside. They would need their sunhats today.	
Some people like getting up early. Others prefer to stay up late.	
They went to the museum. It was raining all day, so it was the best option.	

Extension Write two to three sentences of your own with semicolons.

Using the senses to create mood and atmosphere in writing

When the author is lost in the darkness in 'Finding our way through the dark', she describes the noises she hears.

- Imagine listening to the amplified sounds in the dark of the night. Perhaps they are the sounds of nature, or the sound of the city at night. Write about what you hear and feel, using descriptive language so that your reader feels like they are there themselves.

Extension Think of another place or thing to describe in a piece of writing using superlatives, a description of the senses, and semicolons to help structure your writing.

Writing about a future day in your life

You have written an account of a day you experienced in the past (Student Book page 31). Now it's time to look to the future!

- Write about a day you would like to have in the future, considering the following:
  - When will your special day be, and where?
  - What activities will you do?
  - Who will you be with?
  - How do you think you will feel?
  - Make it as inventive and imaginative as you like!

Designing a promotional poster

- Design a poster to promote an event in the area you live in. Consider the following:

  ○ What event will you choose? It could be a summer music festival, a school play, a sponsored walk, a dance show or something entirely different!

  ○ What text will you include on the poster? How will you present it to highlight the most important information?

  ○ How will you use graphics and colour to make your poster eye-catching?

Disturbing place names

The extract 'A day trip on the Moon' on pages 36–38 of your Student Book includes some disturbing place names, such as the 'Sea of Thirst' and the 'Mountains of Inaccessibility'.

- Invent your own disturbing place name, such as 'Sea of …', 'Mountain of …', 'Valley of …', 'Ocean of …', 'Tree of …' or 'Desert of …', and then write a paragraph to describe this unusual place and how it got its name.

Opposite forms in language

Many words can take on the opposite meaning when one of the following prefixes is applied: *dis-, in-, un-*.

Examples: 'disjointed', 'inexcusable', 'unknown'

- Now choose the appropriate prefix to change the word in brackets and complete the sentences.

The calculations were *(correct)* _____incorrect_____.

He was *(able)* _____ to attend the meeting.

She was *(attentive)* _____ and did not reply.

I'm sorry but I *(agree)* _____ with you about this.

His *(appearance)* _____ was a mystery to all.

Hurricanes are *(common)* _____ in England.

Extension Now write your own sentences using your favourite *dis-, in-* and *un-* words.

In this unit, you will examine the differences between British and American English, and the English where you live, practise contractions and adverbs, revise complex and compound sentences, and write a variety of text types including an autobiography and a playscript.

Vocabulary: English in different countries

Most countries in the world base their standard English use on either British or American English.

- Look at the table below and draw a line to match each British English word to its American equivalent.

British English	American English	English where you live
holiday	sidewalk	
mum	elevator	
flat	vacation	
pavement	trunk	
boot (of a car)	apartment	
trainers	subway	
jumper	cookie	
biscuit	sneakers	
aeroplane	mom	
underground	sweater	
lorry	truck	
lift	soccer	
football	airplane	

- Write in the third column the words you are most likely to use where you live. Each one could be British, American or a different word altogether!

Extension Write a paragraph that includes three or four of the words used where you live.

Pronoun and verb contraction revision

The most common form of contraction is the pairing of a subject pronoun with a modal verb. Below are some of the pronouns and verbs that can be easily contracted in English.

- Create pairs of subject pronouns and verbs from the list below. Write the contraction alongside each pair.
  Subject pronouns: *I, we, you, they, she, he, it*
  Verbs: *are, had, has, have, is, shall, was, were, will, would*

Subject pronoun + verb	Contraction
we are	we're

You're the editor!

- The following paragraph has many mistakes in spelling, grammar, and punctuation. Find the errors and correct as many as you can.

I expect my education to provide me with the exspertise to be successful in the future.

This includes developing strong skills in the basics reading, writing, and arithmatics. To often

i here students complaining that a lesson is boring but uninteresting. My friend Sally believes

that mathematics will play know roll in her life, i think that is a mistake! At the same time its

important for education to provide opportunitys to explore and develope talents and abilities

not directly related to the basic skills.

Extension Add another sentence or two to your corrected text, explaining what you think is needed from education today.

Complex and compound sentences

Here are some theories on the value of education expressed through complex and compound sentences.

- Join the correct sentence halves together.

There are many different stages or types of education	by which we really mean painful experience – that does the bulk of the instruction for us.
School is meant to teach us what we need to know to live and yet it is most often life –	opinions about what is needed to provide a good education.
In most parts of the world, providing a good education	that contribute to lifelong learning.
Although it may not seem like a complicated issue, there are so many different theories and	a computer and the internet?
How important is it for every child to have access to	is seen as essential to society and personal wellbeing.

Ordering content

- Rearrange these sentences, by numbering them from 1 to 6, to tell the story of the unruly donkey in Nelson Mandela's autobiography on pages 51–52 of your Student Book. Number 1 has been done for you.

It bent its head, trying to unseat me, which it did, but not before the thorns had pricked and scratched my face, embarrassing me in front of my friends.	
Even though it was a donkey that unseated me, I learned that to humiliate another person is to make him suffer an unnecessarily cruel fate.	
I learned my lesson one day from an unruly donkey.	I
Even as a boy, I defeated my opponents without dishonouring them.	
Africans have a highly developed sense of dignity.	
We had been taking turns climbing up and down its back and when my chance came, I jumped on, and the donkey bolted into a nearby thorn bush.	

Extension Which of the sentences on this page are complex sentences and which are compound sentences? Explain your answers.

Autobiography writing

What were your early school days like? Prepare to write a four-paragraph essay about your early school experiences.

● Fill in the chart below with as much as you can remember.

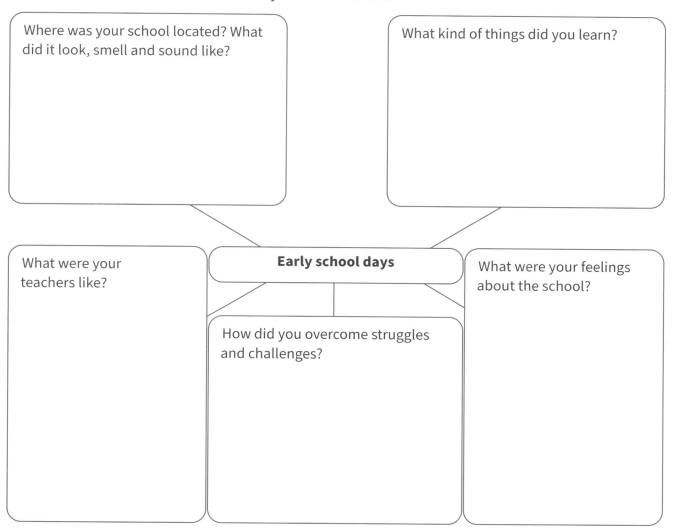

Where was your school located? What did it look, smell and sound like?

What kind of things did you learn?

What were your teachers like?

Early school days

What were your feelings about the school?

How did you overcome struggles and challenges?

● Now use your notes and the suggested structure below to help you write an essay entitled 'My Early School Days' in the space provided on the next page.

Paragraph 1	Introduction: introduce the topic and explain where your school was.
Paragraph 2	Explain the kind of things you learned and what your teachers were like.
Paragraph 3	Describe any struggles or challenges you had and how you tackled them. Describe your feelings and give examples.
Paragraph 4	Conclusion: conclude by describing the impact your early school days have had on you.

My Early School Days

Descriptive writing

- Prepare to write a detailed description of the first place you remember living in by making notes on:

What the place looked, sounded and smelled like
Who you might see outside
The wider area: what was immediately around where you lived?

- Use your notes to write a paragraph that describes this place in detail. Aim to create a clear image in the reader's mind. Make sure you include compound sentences using conjunctions such as 'yet', 'and', 'but', 'nor' and 'for'.

Creating -ly adverbs

Adverbs modify verbs, adjectives or other adverbs. They often end in the suffix -ly.

Modifying a verb: Salim sings <u>beautifully</u>.

Modifying an adjective: Akari is <u>extremely</u> clever.

Modifying an adverb: This train is going <u>incredibly</u> fast.

Some -ly words are adjectives, such as 'friendly' or 'lively'.

- Choose a noun or verb from the list and create an -ly adverb to complete each sentence:

bad, careful, expert, infuriating, ~~impatient~~, quick, uncomfortable

She was hungry and waited for her food _____*impatiently*_____.

He found the puzzle _____ difficult.

A forest fire can spread _____.

It was _____ hot in summer.

The _____ written document supported her case.

The children were behaving _____.

They walked down the steep hill _____.

Plan your own playscript

- Prepare to write a scene in which the characters are having a conversation about education. Make notes on:

  ○ Characters: are they students, teachers, parents, politicians …?

  ○ Key roles: brief description of their backgrounds and personal attributes

  ○ Setting: is it in a school or public institution? In a specific city or country?

Write your playscript

- Write your short script here. Use contractions and informal language to make it sound like real dialogue. To focus the scene on a dramatic concluding punchline, try writing the last line first.

4 Work

In this unit, you will practise prepositions, colloquial language, the third conditional form and the use of the passive voice. You will write a paragraph, draft interview questions, write a job profile and write a summary.

Writing a paragraph

● What kind of work would you like to do when you complete your education? Do you have a job now? Write a paragraph to describe either the work you would like to do later or the job you have now.

Start with a topic sentence which gives the main idea of the paragraph, followed by at least five sentences with more information, as well as a conclusion.

Vocabulary

● Find a synonym for these phrases with the following vocabulary from 'The kitchen' (pages 58–59 of your Student Book):

contend with, suppress, recuperate, ~~venerable~~, simultaneous

commanding respect _____ venerable _____

strive against or compete _____

restore one's health _____

happening at the same time _____

put an end to forcibly _____

Extension Write about your first day at work, either real or imaginary. Make it dramatic like 'The kitchen'.

Interview research for a job profile

- Interview someone you know about their job and make notes in the space below on what they tell you. Prepare some interview questions in advance. You might ask them about an average day, how they got the job, and what they like and dislike about it.

Writing your job profile

- Now write out the profile, using your findings from the interview. You might begin your introductory paragraph with an interesting quotation or fact.

Prepositions review

- Write the missing prepositions from 'Sky high: the air traffic controller' on pages 61–62 of your Student Book in the text below.

And though Evans seems a master _____of_____ it now, she only got _____

air traffic control, quite literally, _____ accident. All set to join the army

_____ university, she snapped a ligament in her knee and was rejected

_____ medical grounds. _____ she was looking around

_____ alternatives, a friend who had already begun training _____

a controller recommended the air traffic service. "And the more I read about it," she says "the

more I thought, ooh, that sounds right _____ my street."

Colloquial language

- Read the colloquial phrases from 'Painting the fence' on pages 65–68 of your Student Book in the first column and rewrite them using Standard English in the second column.

Why, ain't that work?	Isn't that work?
You see, Aunt Polly's awful particular about this fence	
… you don't mean to let on that you like it?	
I'd let you, if you was me, Tom.	
You're up a stump, ain't you!	
Now don't you see how I'm fixed?	
Why, it's you, Ben! I warn't noticing.	

Extension Write five sentences using colloquial expressions that you often hear. Explain their meanings.

The third conditional

The third conditional is used to describe situations that are no longer possible. These are **imaginary past actions**.

The basic pattern is:
'If' ... + past perfect ... 'would' + 'have' + past participle

Towards the end of the story 'Painting the fence', Tom considers what happened and what could have happened had the situation been different. Tom realizes that it is too late to change anything.

'If he <u>hadn't run</u> out of whitewash, he <u>would have bankrupted</u> every boy in the village.' (But he did run out of whitewash, so he couldn't bankrupt anyone.)

'If he <u>had been</u> a great and wise philosopher, like the writer of this book, he <u>would</u> now <u>have comprehended</u> that Work consists of whatever a body is obliged to do ...' (But he was not a great and wise philosopher.)

- Complete these sentences in the third conditional using this pattern.

If you hadn't studied harder, you would have failed the exam.
If I had known you were coming, I
If you hadn't told me that before, I
If he had kept a record of his fastest running time, he
If we had looked at the weather forecast, we

Extension Write three third conditional sentences of your own.

Writing a summary

● Make notes on what you can remember about the key characters and events in 'Painting the fence' (Student Book pages 65–68). Use these notes to write a summary that focuses on the most significant parts of the story.

The passive voice

The passive voice is useful when we want to put the focus on the action instead of who or what is doing or causing it.

The basic pattern is: **a form of 'to be' + past participle**

'English <u>is spoken</u> all over the world.'
'The windows <u>have been opened</u>.'

Look at this example of an active sentence:
'The children <u>ate</u> all the crisps in the bowl.'

Here it is in passive form:
'All the crisps in the bowl <u>were eaten</u> by the children.'

Notice how the subject of the sentence and the verb form change.

● Now change the following sentences from active voice into passive voice.

Thousands of tourists visit the Grand Canyon every year.

_____

Someone ate my sandwich yesterday.

_____

The changes to the curriculum affected the students.

_____

Someone stole my laptop when I went out for a quick break.

_____

5 The weather

In this unit, you will revise the use of dashes, brackets and reported speech, write about the weather using descriptive detail, and write an extended metaphor poem.

The single dash

A single dash can be used in place of other types of punctuation to add extra information to a sentence in a final clause. It can be more dynamic and informal than other breaking punctuation like colons or semicolons.

Look at these examples. The second one is the way it appears in 'A frozen world':

"Don't worry, it's quite warm today. Just wait till it gets really cold!"

"Don't worry, it's quite warm today – just wait till it gets really cold!"

- Rewrite the following sentences as a sentence that ends in a dash clause.

I awoke to the sounds of hail beating on the tin roof. I was glad to have shelter.

I awoke to the sounds of hail beating on the tin roof – I was glad to have shelter.

She was afraid of two things: lightning and being called up at school assembly.

_____

_____

They took an umbrella with them; it looked like it might rain.

_____

_____

He was incredibly tall. He must have been the tallest person she had ever seen.

_____

_____

She wants the money; she wants it now.

_____

_____

Extension Now write three sentences of your own that use a single dash before the final clause.

Using brackets (parentheses)

Brackets (or parentheses) can add a detail, date span, reference or side point to a sentence.

Examples:
'I have two parents (Mahia and Ahmad) and three sisters (Joyah, Siti and Nayla).'
'Abraham Lincoln (1809–1865) was the sixteenth president of the United States.'
'She said she liked the gift (I don't think she did).'

● Complete the following sentences by inserting brackets in appropriate places in each one.

William Shakespeare 1564–1616 was an English playwright, poet and actor.

I have two cats Luna and Molly and a rabbit Max.

Amala's parents said they would drive me home they just live in the next suburb.

Dashes in pairs

Dashes used in pairs can provide additional information in the middle of a sentence, such as in the following sentence from 'A frozen world':

Everything, and I mean everything – my water, tomato paste, soap – is encased in thick, milky ice.

If this additional clause was removed, the sentence would still make sense:
'Everything, and I mean everything, is encased in thick, milky ice.'

● Rewrite the following sentences so the additional clause in brackets is included between dashes.

She ran fast and managed to catch him. (faster than ever before)

She ran fast – faster than ever before – and managed to catch him.

There wasn't much on offer for breakfast and I was very hungry. (only fruit and tea)

_____

The supermarket is on the retail park. (which is the largest one in the town)

_____

Extension Now write two sentences of your own using brackets and two more using pairs of dashes.

Vocabulary: 'A frozen world'

- Match the following words to their meanings.

remote	to be brave enough to go somewhere
surrounding	hidden
to venture	to bounce off a surface
gradually	to kill an animal for food
concealed	unable to feel
to jostle	the area around
to ricochet	to keep something in good condition
numb	far away
to slaughter	to push someone roughly
to preserve	happening slowly

Descriptive detail

Descriptive detail makes writing more compelling. For example, in 'A frozen world' on pages 74–76 of your Student Book, the author uses the phrases 'thick, milky ice' and 'steaming black coffee'.

- Complete the following phrases describing aspects of the scenery or weather choosing appropriate adjectives, adverbs and punctuation.

The _____ clouds
The _____ of air
The water's _____ surface
The _____ evening light
A _____ river
_____ waves
A _____ wind
_____ flashes of lightning

Extension Write three more sentences of your own to describe the weather or scenery in descriptive detail.

Writing an extended metaphor poem

- Use the boxes below to help you plan your own extended metaphor. Instead of using zoomorphism, as you did in the Student Book activity, try to come up with a different subject to create your extended metaphor. Perhaps a particular person, a form of transport, or a city. Then turn your notes into a poem, using 'Fog' on page 78 of your Student Book as a model.

Type of weather:

Three ways that the two are compared:
-
-
-

What you are comparing it to:

- Now write your poem in the space below.

Reported speech: 'The storm'

We can quote someone directly: "It is a beautiful painting," she said.

Or we can use reported speech: 'She said it was a beautiful painting.'

Notice how 'is' changes to 'was' for reported speech. When using reported speech, we have to move one tense back in time:

present simple	⟹	past simple
present continuous	⟹	past continuous
past simple	⟹	past perfect
present perfect	⟹	past perfect
present perfect continuous	⟹	past perfect continuous

In 'The storm' on pages 83–85 of your Student Book, reported speech is used: 'The older people said that there was a storm coming.'

This is told in the past tense, so we know that the original sentence must have been: "There is a storm coming," they said.

- Change the following sentences from the text into reported speech.

"I don't see any clouds," said Mehmet.

Mehmet said he didn't see any clouds.

"I've known it was coming for a long time," she said.

_____

"But you can't see the wind," replied Mehmet.

_____

- Now change these sentences from reported speech into direct speech.

Mehmet said there was no storm coming.

_____

Muhlis said it was the dirt and dust caught up in the wind.

_____

Zekiye told them she had bread, olives and fruit.

_____

Extension Write your own sentence with direct speech and then change your sentence into reported speech. Do the same the other way round with a different sentence.

Vocabulary: 'The storm'

- Complete the following sentences with the correct form of the words below.

rake, knock, soak, plague, search, rustle

By day they were _____plagued_____ with flies.

At lunch-time they _____ on the door and fetched their tray of bread, olives and fruit and _____ for the shade.

After lunch they _____ the grass into a pile.

Another gust _____ the leaves in the garden.

They _____ their heads and shirts with water from the hose.

The words listed below are all found in the extract 'The storm'. They are synonyms for the words and phrases listed in the first column of the table.

- Write the synonym for each word or phrase in the second column.

hastily, gust, barefoot, stumble, heap, leapt, flung, crawl

- Then write in the third column the word class for each one.

Word/phrase	Synonym from 'The storm'	Word class
without shoes	barefoot	adjective
to move on hands and knees		
to almost fall		
pile		
sharp blast of wind		
thrown		
hurriedly		
jumped		

Extension Write sentences of your own with each of the synonyms above and using a variety of punctuation.

6 Being free

In this unit, you will revise 'If only …' and 'I wish …', conjunctive adverbs, possessives and abstract nouns. You will write poetry and texts considering different situations and points of view.

Your secret country

- Write a further seven-line stanza to come after the concluding lines of the poem you read on page 88 of your Student Book:

> In that secret country
> Which is your country and mine.

Use rhythm, rhyme, repetition and flow to expand upon the possibilities of this unnamed country that is 'your country and mine' by completing the following with lines of your own. The first and last lines are already written for you.

> In my secret country
> It's a …
>
>
> It's a …
>
>
> There are …
>
>
> There is …
>
>
> And …
>
>
> And it's your country and mine.

Extension Write a short poem about your idea of a free country using a different rhyme scheme to the one you used in the activity above.

'If only …' and 'I wish …' phrases

We use 'If only …' to express feelings about the past, present and future. 'If Only Papa Hadn't Danced', the title of the short story which the extract 'A dangerous border crossing' comes from (on pages 90–92 of your Student Book), gives an example of feelings about the past.

The phrases 'If only …' and 'I wish …' can be used in a similar way, but 'If only …' is stronger than 'I wish …'.

- Rewrite each of these sentences twice using 'I wish …' and 'If only …'.

My education did not prepare me for this.	If only my education had prepared me for this. I wish that my education had prepared me for this.
I don't have a bicycle, so I have to catch the bus.	
We never go to exciting places for our holidays.	
I wanted to walk out and never come back.	
The gate wasn't shut properly.	

- Think of situations where you wished things were different. Maybe you wish you had said something different, or acted in a different way. Write your own 'If only …' and 'I wish …' sentences to reflect this.

Vocabulary: 'A dangerous border crossing'

● Write down the meanings of the verbs underlined below in your own words.

She gestured to the tawny hills across the river.	to move an arm or your head to show something
That night, we hid in the bushes.	
We would wade across at midnight, when the man in the orange jumpsuit had gone home.	
my nerve would fail if I faltered for even a moment	
He didn't say a word, just lifted me up onto his shoulders and strode into the water.	
Once more Papa stepped into the river – this time to fetch our suitcase.	
Finally Papa emerged from the darkness.	
Mama wailed piteously.	
I scrambled through the fence.	

Writing from another point of view

- 'A dangerous border crossing' is told from the viewpoint of a young girl. Now think about the viewpoint of the man in the orange jumpsuit. What is his backstory? Write an opening paragraph for his story. The opening phrase is provided.

I was out there early to patrol the fence, and soon after I got there I saw ...

Extension Write further paragraphs to expand on your backstory for the man in the orange jumpsuit.

Conjunctive adverbs that go with semicolons

When a conjunctive adverb is used to connect independent clauses as one sentence, you should put a semicolon before it and a comma after it, as with this example:
'You must do the revision to catch up with the class; otherwise, you will fail.'

Note: You can also write this as two separate sentences:
'You must do the revision to catch up with the class. Otherwise, you will fail.'

- Choose the most appropriate conjunctive adverb from the list below to complete the following sentences.

otherwise, besides, consequently, eventually, finally, instead

He couldn't bring himself to tell the truth; _____ *instead* _____, he lied.
The tree was split by lightning; _____, it will have to be cut down.
She needs to leave in five minutes; _____, she'll be late for school.
They looked into his business operations; _____, he was charged with fraud.
Seeing his wide eyes, she gave him her lunch; _____, she wasn't really hungry.
They had all been safely returned home; _____, it was over.

Practising possessives

A singular word will have an apostrophe and then an 's' to indicate the possessive.
For example: 'teacher's books' (just one teacher)

A plural word will have an added 's' to indicate the plural, and then an apostrophe.
For example: 'teachers' books' (more than one teacher)

A plural word that does not need an 's' for the plural will have an apostrophe and then an 's' for the possessive.
For example: 'women's jackets' (more than one woman, but *'s* not *s'*)

- Place an apostrophe in each of the following phrases.

The childrens voices	Her neighbours friend	The womens group
Dr Flints property	Peoples rights	The mens chatter
The neighbours voices (plural)	A womans letter	The workers union (plural)

Extension Write your own sentence that includes a single and a plural possessive.

Abstract nouns

Abstract nouns describe ideas, qualities or states, rather than physical objects. They are often used to draw people's attention to important issues like human rights.

- Match the following abstract nouns in the first column to their meanings in the second column.

authority		being free and independent with unrestricted movement
autonomy		hiding someone or something or keeping a secret
concealment		freedom from control or imprisonment, right to self-direction
democracy		reliance on one's own abilities and resources
freedom		a government of representatives elected by the people
incarceration		the right or power to give orders, or make something happen
liberty		governing a country or treating somebody cruelly or unjustly
oppression		self-government, freedom to act as you want to
self-reliance		being shut up, imprisoned or confined in a building like a jail

Your idea of freedom

- Now that you have considered some of the terms used to discuss ideas of freedom or its opposite condition (not being free), write about your own idea of freedom in the box below. Use as many abstract nouns as you can.

Vocabulary: 'The loophole of retreat'

- The following phrases appear in 'The loophole of retreat' on pages 97–99 of your Student Book. Write a synonym for each of the underlined words below.

a <u>concealed</u> trap-door	hidden
I was <u>weary,</u> and I slept	
This continued darkness was <u>oppressive</u>	
I was never <u>lacerated</u> with the whip from head to foot	
I <u>toiled</u> in the fields from morning till night	
my aunt Nancy would <u>seize</u> such opportunities	
I had a shuddering, superstitious feeling that it was a <u>bad omen</u>	
the <u>scorching</u> summer's sun	
the <u>tedious</u> monotony of my life	
the cold penetrated through the thin shingle roof, and I was <u>dreadfully</u> chilled	
no thoughts to occupy my mind, except the <u>dreary</u> past	
I heard slave-hunters planning how to catch some poor <u>fugitive</u>	
Several times I heard <u>allusions</u> to Dr Flint	

Extension Write a sentence that includes at least three of the words underlined in the first column above.

7 The future

In this unit, you will revise different types of adverbs, word classes and the passive, and practise using persuasive language and poetic devices. You will write to yourself from the future, write your own science fiction and write a descriptive passage.

Powerful poetry, prose and speech

As you will have read in 'I have a dream', 'I, too, sing America' and 'Dear Matafele Peinam' on pages 107 and 109 of your Student Book, powerful or persuasive writing requires direct language and an expression of commitment.

- Complete each of the following sentences in your own words. Choose language that creates impact and expresses commitment to a cause.

I have a dream that one day …
I, too …
We will work together to …

Words that create impact

The vocabulary used by Martin Luther King, Jr., along with other rhetorical devices, in his 'I have a dream' speech results in maximum impact on the listener. You read part of this speech on page 106 of your Student Book.

- Write in your own words the meanings of the words below.

sweltering	extremely or stiflingly hot
injustice	
oasis	
despair	
discord	
symphony	
struggle	

Some poetic devices

Here are some examples of useful poetic devices that are discussed in this unit.

Alliteration

Alliteration is the repetition of letters or sounds at the beginning of closely placed words, as in this extract from the poem 'I, too, sing America' by Langston Hughes.

> When company comes

- Now write your own lines using alliteration.

Enjambment

Enjambment means the continuation of a sentence from one line of poetry to the next without the use of any punctuation, as in this extract from 'I, too, sing America':

> Nobody'll dare
> Say to me [...]

- Now write your own lines using enjambment.

Free verse

Free verse follows the natural rhythms of speech, as in this extract from the poem 'Dear Matafele Peinam' by Kathy Jetñil-Kijiner:

> we are
> petitions blooming
> from
> teenage fingertips

- Now write your own lines using free verse.

Extension Find another poetic device that is used in this unit, and write your own lines using this device, as in the activity above.

Circumstantial adverbs

Circumstantial adverbs give us more detail about a verb. They fall into several categories, including: frequency, manner, place, and time. Test for these types by asking **'How often?'** for frequency, **'How?'** for manner, **'Where?'** for place, and **'When?'** for time.

- Identify the adverb types below by putting an **F** (frequency), **M** (manner), **P** (place), or **T** (time) after each one.

never F	outside	wrongly	after dark
down the road	twice	fast	soon enough
noisily	very often	happily	underwater

- Write three sentences using at least one of these adverbs in each one.

> Despite the freezing weather, she still went outside.

Adverbs of frequency

Here are some examples of adverbs and adverbial phrases of time and frequency:

often, rarely, usually, eventually, frequently, hardly ever, occasionally

- Write four sentences choosing from the above adverbs and adverbial phrases to describe what you do or don't do.

> I often go swimming on a Saturday.

Extension Write a longer sentence that includes at least three different types of adverb.

Word class revision

- Sort the following powerful words from 'My return' (pages 111–113 of your Student Book) into the verb/noun/adjective/adverb columns below.
  Note: Some words can belong to more than one word class.

inky, blackness, brightly, ebb, steadily, overhead, starless, glowing, scarlet, motionless, harsh, reddish, intensely, vegetation, perpetual, twilight, horizon, stirring, pale, incrustation, convey, fitfully, swaying, lurid, monstrous, antennae, gleaming, threadlike, abominable, desolation, sombre, contributed, appalling, westward, extinct, aghast, eclipse, northward, obscure, eddying, distinctly, smeared

- Then add as many synonyms as you can think of for these words to the table.

Verb	Noun	Adjective	Adverb
ebb	blackness	inky	brightly

Writing science fiction

● If you have already written about a dystopian future (Student Book page 114), this time write a utopian scenario, and vice versa. Be descriptive and dramatic!

Extension Write three to four sentences using words from the table in the word class revision activity on page 47.

Finding and using adjectives

In 'My return' on pages 111–113 of your Student Book, the writer uses rich adjectives to describe the landscape and the creature.

- Underline the adjectives and choose five examples to use in your own writing.

> I stopped and sat upon the Time Machine, looking around. The sky was no longer <u>blue</u>. Ahead, it was inky dark, and out of the blackness shone brightly and steadily the white stars. Overhead it was starless and a deep red and behind it was glowing scarlet where lay the huge sun, red and motionless. The rocks about me were of a harsh reddish colour, and all the trace of life that I could see at first was the intensely green vegetation that covered every projecting point. It was the same rich green that one sees on plants which grow in a perpetual twilight.

- Write a short descriptive passage using the five adjectives you chose from the extract above.

Adding *-ness* to create a noun

Many adjectives can be changed into nouns by adding the suffix *-ness*. A noun ending in *-ness* means the state of the original adjective: the noun 'emptiness', as found in 'A superior robot' (pages 115–118 of your Student Book) is the state of being 'empty'.

- Change the adjectives below into nouns and then complete the sentences below:

tidy, happy, bright, dark, sad

> When she heard that her friend was leaving, Emily was filled with _____ sadness _____.
>
> Hurray, we passed the exams! We are filled with _____.
>
> When the street lights went out we were surrounded by _____.
>
> In the summer we often need sunglasses to cope with the _____ of the sun.
>
> I can't stand mess; _____ is very important to me.

Extension Try to think of three other nouns ending in *-ness* and write sentences that include them.

Attributive and predicative adjectives

Adjectives can be placed either before or after the noun that they refer to.
Attributive adjectives appear before a noun, for example, 'a <u>cold</u> day'.
Predicative adjectives appear after a noun, for example, 'the day was <u>cold</u>'.

- Identify the adjectives in the quotation from 'A superior robot' and state whether they are attributive or predicative in the sentence.

He placed a hand upon Cutie's steel shoulder and the metal was cold and hard to the touch.	
Adjective:	Attributive or predicative:
Adjective:	Attributive or predicative:
Adjective:	Attributive or predicative:

Revising the passive

We use the passive when we want to focus on the action being done rather than who or what is doing it: 'The first industrial robot, Unimate, was built in 1961.'

Look at this example of an active sentence:
'In 1843, Ada Lovelace published an article imagining the first computer programme.'

Here is how it could be written in passive form:
'In 1843, an article imagining the first computer programme was published by Ada Lovelace.'

Do you notice that the subject of the active sentence, Ada Lovelace, is no longer the subject of the verb in the passive sentence? However, it is not always necessary to say who carried out the action. For example, we could also say, 'In 1843, an article imagining the first computer programme was published.'

- Change these active sentences into the passive. They are all in the simple past tense.

Martin Luther King, Jr. made the powerful speech 'I have a dream' in 1963.

Langston Hughes wrote the poem 'I, too, sing America' in 1944.

Karel Čapek first used the word 'robot' in a play in 1920.

George Devol invented the first modern robot in 1954.

Write to yourself from the future!

You have already written about your vision of the future (Student Book page 120), and what you think society, technology and the environment will be like in your chosen future time.

- Imagine you have been transported to this point in the future. Write a message, email or other type of communication (perhaps a futuristic one that doesn't exist yet) back to yourself in the present day. What is a typical day like? What things are better or worse? Do you find anything amusing/scary/worrying? What do you think society today should be doing differently to ensure this future scenario does or doesn't happen?

8 A dream of flying

In this unit, you will revise the passive, and metaphors and similes; write a summary, an opinion essay and a dramatic account; think about paragraph titles, and learn about verbs with the infinitive and *-ing* form.

Finding information | You will need SB p122

- Reread the first two paragraphs from the story of 'Daedalus and Icarus'. Complete the boxes below by filling in the missing information.

When Talos was twelve years old … he had better skills as an inventor than Daedalus.
Talos studied …
He invented …
And he also invented …
Daedalus became …
He invited Talos …
He pushed Talos …
He tried to bury …
Talos's soul …
The partridge …

Extension Write your own summary analysis of a (mythical) flying hero.

Summary writing | You will need SB pp122–124 |

Read the story of 'Daedalus and Icarus' again, from the point where Daedalus flees to Crete with his son (the third paragraph).

- Write the main events of the story as bullet points.

- When you are sure that you have all of the most important points, write a summary of the story in your own words.

Revising the passive (continued from Unit 7, page 49)

- Change these sentences from the active to the passive form.

> Daedalus took on his nephew, Talos, as an apprentice.
>
> <u>Talos was taken on as an apprentice by his Uncle Daedalus.</u>
>
> Daedalus devised an evil plan.
>
> _____
>
> It was not easy to escape Crete because it was an island.
>
> _____

- Change these sentences from the passive to the active form.

> The first saw was invented by Talos.
>
> _____
>
> The labyrinth was built by Daedalus.
>
> _____
>
> Talos was buried where he fell (by the Greeks).
>
> _____

Writing your opinion: essay

You are going to write an opinion essay on the following topic: *Flying inventions pre-twentieth century: foolish or inspired?*

Look at the structure below to give you an idea of what you will need to include.

Paragraph 1 (introduction)	Capture your audience. Ask a question <u>or</u> state an amazing fact while introducing the topic.
Paragraph 2 (main body)	Discuss your first viewpoint with examples and evidence. Balance reasoning and factual information.
Paragraph 3 (main body)	Discuss your second viewpoint with examples and evidence.
Paragraph 4 (main body)	Think of an opposing viewpoint to argue against your other viewpoints, with examples and evidence.
Paragraph 5 (conclusion)	Restate your opinion in a different way.

Continued on the following page

Extension Write a sentence of your own in the passive form that relates to the story of 'Daedalus and Icarus'. Then rewrite the sentence in the active form.

Planning your essay

- Conduct some research into earlier designs for human flight, thinking about both the risks and the benefits. What is your viewpoint? Fill in the table below in preparation to write your opinion essay.

Viewpoint		**Reasons**
	$\Rightarrow$	
	$\Rightarrow$	
	$\Rightarrow$	

Write your essay

- Now write up your essay using your planning notes on page 54 and the structure on page 53.

Vocabulary: 'Flying into Alicante'

- The sentences below are from 'Flying into Alicante' on page 130 of your Student Book. Replace the underlined word with a synonym or short phrase that has the same meaning.

like a <u>torrent</u> under a bridge	rushing water
his limbs still <u>quivering</u>	
the same vision <u>hovers</u> before his gaze	
a <u>radiant</u> landscape	
with a sudden <u>certitude</u>	

Metaphor and simile: 'Flying into Alicante'

- The paragraphs below contain a number of similes and metaphors. Underline the similes in red and the metaphors in green.

> From up there the earth had looked bare and dead; but as the plane loses altitude, it robes itself in colours. The woods spread out their quilts, the hills and valleys rise and fall in waves, like someone breathing. A mountain over which he flies swells like some recumbent giant's breast, almost grazing his wing-tip.
>
> Now close, like a torrent under a bridge, the earth begins its mad acceleration. The ordered world becomes a landslide, as houses and villages are torn from the smooth horizon and swept away behind him.

Metaphors and similes are comparisons between two things.

- Choose one metaphor and one simile from the paragraphs above and explain what two things are being compared in each case.

Metaphor:
Simile:

Extension Write a sentence of your own that includes a metaphor. Then rewrite your sentence changing your metaphor into a simile. Which do you think works better?

Writing about a dramatic experience

Think of a dramatic scenario that involves someone taking on some kind of extreme risk or challenge. Perhaps it is an accident, a weather incident, some kind of equipment failure or just something they attempted in order to fulfil a dream (like flying).

- Make notes on specific details in the space below to prepare to write up an account of the dramatic scenario.

Name and age of the person, their skills, interests and where they live.
How they came to be at the particular time and place of the action.
The dramatic or dangerous events that occurred.
What they did to achieve a good outcome.
The literary devices you will use to enhance your writing.

Writing up your experience

● Use your notes from the previous page to write up your account.

Paragraph titles You will need SB pp132–134

- Reread the first four paragraphs of 'Hassan' carefully. Look for the main idea and think of an appropriate title for each paragraph, writing them in the space below.

Paragraph 1 title: Main idea:
Paragraph 2 title: Main idea:
Paragraph 3 title: Main idea:
Paragraph 4 title: Main idea:

Character description

- Read the text again and see how many references to Hassan you can find. Based on these references, what do you think Hassan looks like? What about his personality? Write a description of Hassan in the box below.

Verbs with the infinitive

When certain verbs are followed by another verb, this needs to be an infinitive.
Some common verbs which take this form are:

afford, agree, appear, arrange, attempt, dare, decide, fail, forget, hope,
learn (how), manage, offer, plan, pretend, promise, refuse, seem, tend, threaten

verb + infinitive ('to' + root form of the verb)
'The boys <u>managed to fly</u> their kite the furthest.'

● Complete the following sentences with the **infinitive ('to' + root form of the verb)**.

Hassan and I decided …	We agreed …
People gathered on the sidewalks and roofs …	I promise …

Verbs with the *-ing* form

If a verb follows any of the verbs listed below, it will take the *-ing* form.

avoid, consider, delay, deny, enjoy, finish, imagine, involve, mind, miss, postpone,
practise, regret, risk, stop, suggest

verb + *-ing* form
'She <u>enjoyed watching</u> the film.'

● Complete the following sentences with verbs in the *-ing* form.

Didn't the thief deny …	Would you consider …
I don't mind …	Stop …

Now test yourself!

● Choose the correct verb form and complete the sentences.

Hassan planned …	Icarus enjoyed …
One day Hassan and I would learn …	King Minos was so rich he could afford …

Extension Write two sentences of your own that take the **verb + infinitive** form
and two sentences that take the **verb + *-ing*** form.

9 Cities

In this unit, you will practise analyzing data, revise the use of either/neither and personification, complete a cloze exercise, write to convey feeling, and write an extended description.

Analyzing data

- Look at the charts and analyze their data. Using your analysis of the data provided, write five bullet points to discuss your findings. Use compare and contrast phrases like 'more than', 'less than', 'fewer than', 'the most', and 'the least'.

The 10 largest cities in 1000	
1 Córdoba, Spain	450,000
2 Kaifeng, China	400,000
3 Constantinople (Istanbul), Turkey	300,000
4 Angkor, Cambodia	200,000
5 Kyoto, Japan	175,000
6 Cairo, Egypt	135,000
7 Baghdad, Iraq	125,000
8 Nishapur (Neyshabur), Iran	125,000
9 Al-Hasa, Saudi Arabia	110,000
10 Patan (Anhilwara), India	100,000

The 10 largest cities in 1500	
1 Beijing, China	672,000
2 Vijayanagar, India	500,000
3 Cairo, Egypt	400,000
4 Hangzhou, China	250,000
5 Tabriz, Iran	250,000
6 Constantinople (Istanbul), Turkey	200,000
7 Gauḍa, India	200,000
8 Paris, France	185,000
9 Guangzhou, China	150,000
10 Nanjing, China	147,000

The 10 largest cities in 2022	
1 Tokyo, Japan	37,435,191
2 Delhi, India	29,399,141
3 Shanghai, China	26,317,104
4 São Paulo, Brazil	21,846,507
5 Mexico City, Mexico	21,671,908
6 Cairo, Egypt	20,484,965
7 Dhaka, Bangladesh	20,283,552
8 Mumbai, India	20,185,064
9 Beijing, China	20,035,455
10 Osaka, Japan	19,222,665

Extension Briefly research two more cities, and write two to three sentences to compare and contrast them.

Negative and positive alternatives

Comparison and contrast is often based on a negative or positive approach to an issue:
'Either … or …' is used when making a positive decision between two or more things.
'Neither … nor …' is used when the choice is negative or the person wants to say that more than one thing is not true.

The essay 'Town' on page 137 of your Student Book uses 'neither … nor …' to emphasize what is not being written about:
'I write of Town … not of London or Paris, <u>neither</u> of Venice <u>nor</u> Oxford …'

This sentence uses 'either … or …' to show a positive choice between two things:
'She needed to choose <u>either</u> chocolate <u>or</u> vanilla icing to put on the cake.'

- Write a sentence with the construction 'neither … nor …' and a sentence with the construction 'either … or …'.

'Neither'/'either' as different word classes

Adverbial:
No, <u>neither</u> do I.
I don't like them <u>either</u>.

Adjectival:
They were on <u>either</u> side of the road.
<u>Neither</u> answer is correct.

Determiner:
<u>Either</u> of you are welcome.
<u>Neither</u> of you are welcome.

Pronoun:
Rule: **either/neither + of + noun phrase**
<u>Either</u> of these products will work.
<u>Neither</u> of you are fit enough.

Conjunction:
You can <u>either</u> call or email me.
I will <u>neither</u> call you nor message you.

- Choose three word classes and write examples using 'either' and 'neither'.

Extension Write a paragraph that includes the word classes you didn't use in the activity above.

Vocabulary: 'Polk Street, San Francisco'

- Look at the words in the left-hand column below, which are taken from 'Polk Street, San Francisco' (pages 138–140 of your Student Book) and match them to their meanings.

sidewalk	sleepy
soiled	seriously
heavy-eyed	began
teetering	high-pitched
with gravity	walking in order to be seen
shrill	made dirty
promenading	complete view of an area
commenced	put out (a light)
extinguished	pavement
panorama	moving unsteadily

Revising personification

The author of 'Polk Street, San Francisco' makes effective use of personification to describe the street. This creates a sense of the street as a living being in itself.

- Rewrite each of these sentences from the extract with no personification. Which version of each sentence do you think creates the most interesting effect for the reader?

> '[The street] woke to its work about seven o'clock'
>
> People started work on the street at about seven o'clock.
> _____
>
> 'Between seven and eight the street breakfasted.'
>
> _____
>
> 'Then all at once the street fell quiet.'
>
> _____
>
> 'The street was asleep.'
>
> _____

Extension Write another sentence of your own to describe the street, using personification.

Cloze exercise | You will need SB p143

- Read the first two paragraphs of the extract 'Black and white' on page 143 of your Student Book once more and familiarize yourself with the text. Then close your book and fill in the missing words from the paragraph below using the words from the list.

apartment, avenues, belonging, cloaked, fellowship, gangster, ~~indoors~~, mansions, neglected, neighbourhoods, overwhelming, rushing, street, surfaces, texture

I preferred being _____indoors_____. The _____ below, the _____ beyond, the city's poor _____ seemed as dangerous as those in a black-and-white _____ film. I love the _____ melancholy when I look at the walls of old _____ buildings and the dark _____ of _____, unpainted, fallen-down wooden _____: only in Istanbul have I seen this _____, this shading. When I watch the black-and-white crowds _____ through the darkening streets on a winter evening, I feel a deep sense of _____, almost as if the night has _____ our lives, our streets, our every _____ in a blanket of darkness.

Writing to convey feeling

The extract 'Black and white' conveys the intense feelings the writer has when talking about his early memories of childhood.

- Write a description of somewhere or something that creates similar feelings of intensity for you.

Writing a description

- Choose a city or town to write about. It should be different to the one you wrote about in the Student Book activity on page 148 – perhaps you could choose a city that is completely different from the other one in climate, culture and population. You might need to do some research to gather information on your chosen city.

- Make some notes for each paragraph in the space below.

Introduction: Give the name of your chosen city and the reason for choosing it. Capture your audience's attention by starting with an interesting fact.

Paragraph 1: Provide some general descriptions of the city. Is it in a significant location? What are your general impressions?

Paragraph 2: Describe parts of the city in detail to provide useful information and commentary.

Paragraph 3: How does it compare to other cities, now and in the past. How is it changing?

Conclusion: What is your opinion of the city? Do you or did you like being there or living there?

Extension Use your notes from the activity above to write about your chosen city. It could be a promotional feature or a travel guide article.

10 Making a difference

In this unit, you will practise writing rhetorical questions, using emotive language and idiomatic phrases, and you will prepare notes for a speech.

Rhetorical questions

Rhetorical questions are often used in speeches and texts, as in this appeal by Greta Thunberg from her speech on pages 150–151 in your Student Book:

> And if solutions within this system are so impossible to find then maybe we should change the system itself?

The question is not an invitation for someone else to answer her directly, but more about capturing the interest of her audience and drawing attention to their shared concerns. Rhetorical questions don't generally require an immediate answer.

- Try out these different approaches to writing rhetorical questions by writing your own rhetorical questions following each of the examples provided.

Rhetorical questions with an obvious answer used to emphasize a point. Examples: 'Is rain wet?', 'Are you serious?'

Rhetorical questions that don't have an obvious answer, or at least a clear one. Examples: 'Who knows?', 'Why not?'

Rhetorical questions that are asked in order to be directly answered. Example: 'How would I go about doing that? Well, I would …'

Speech notes

- Using the skills you learned when writing your speech in the Student Book activity on page 152, choose another topic you would like to give a speech on, and fill in the information below.

Summary of my speech:
What motivates me:
Further defining points:
Research required (including key data):
Useful quotations and reference points:

Continued on the following page

Persuasive language (rhetorical questions, useful phrases and keywords):

Concluding remarks:

Idiomatic phrases

Expressions like 'straight from the horse's mouth' are idiomatic. If you haven't heard them before, you can't always understand their meaning from the words used.

- Test your knowledge of some common English idiomatic phrases by matching the following phrases to their correct meanings.

straight from the horse's mouth	an offering of peace
a bolt from the blue	a state of blissful happiness
a kangaroo court	something that spoils things
I can't think straight	something very expensive
once in a blue moon	from someone with direct knowledge of the situation
an olive branch	a surprise, like a bolt of lightning
a fly in the ointment	I can't think properly
to cost an arm and a leg	a rare occurrence
on cloud nine	a sham or mock court

Extension Using your notes from the speech writing activity, write your speech out in full or as bullet points and rehearse your presentation.

Using emotive language

The introduction of 'A fable for tomorrow' by Rachel Carson on pages 153–155 of your Student Book is presented as a fable that marks the turn from the positive to the negative through the use of emotive language.

- Place each of the emotive words in the 'positive' or 'negative' columns alongside the corresponding neutral words.

Positive	Neutral	Negative	Emotive words
harmony	balance	conformity	harmony, conformity
	multitude		excess, abundance
	attracted		delighted, dazzled
	different		special, strange
	well-known		notorious, famous
	unusual		peculiar, extraordinary
	old		traditional, outdated
	march		riot, demonstration
	fighter		terrorist, soldier
	smell		fragrance, stench

- Now choose a positive/neutral/negative set of words from the list above and write three sentences demonstrating their different meanings.

'Translating' the idioms

● Rewrite the following sentences using the actual meaning of the idiomatic phrase. The first one has been done for you.

The parade was moving at a snail's pace.

The parade was moving very slowly.

Good quality clothes don't have to cost an arm and a leg.

_____

Her green fingers made the garden into an urban oasis.

_____

She felt like a fish out of water in her new school in a new city.

_____

The party games broke the ice and soon everyone was laughing.

_____

I wanted it to be a surprise but her sister let the cat out of the bag.

_____

The council has given the green light to build a community garden.

_____

The student was burning the midnight oil to complete the essay.

_____

They had to rack their brains to come up with a solution.

_____

Extension Write five sentences of your own using an idiomatic phrase in each one.

11 Finding your place

In this unit, you will write a dialogue and a letter, practise comparative adjectives and writing from different points of view, and write a text about leaving somewhere.

Writing a dialogue

'Becoming too American' on pages 163–166 of your Student Book uses dialogue tags and action tags (short descriptions that come before or just after dialogue), to create interesting written dialogue:

> "But Uhmma," I beg, following her down the hall to the kitchen. "It is her birthday."

- Imagine a difficult conversation with a friend or family member and write it in the box below. Think of an appropriate location. Use dialogue and action tags, and direct speech.

Extension Read your dialogue aloud and, if possible, make an audio recording that you can listen back to in order to assess the effectiveness of your writing.

Writing a letter to an advice page of a magazine

You are going to write a letter to an advice page of a magazine asking for help with a relationship. Make your letter different to the one you wrote for the Student Book activity on page 166 by choosing an alternative scenario.

● Use the space below to help you structure your letter.

Paragraph 1: Describe the problems you are having and explain why the relationship is important to you.

Paragraph 2: Provide some examples of difficult situations and how you have tried to resolve them.

Paragraph 3: Conclude by explaining the difference it would make in your life to improve this important relationship.

Extension Write a short response from the magazine's advice page to the letter you wrote above.

Comparative adjectives

The opening line of the extract 'Learning the English' (pages 167–169 of your Student Book) uses comparative adjectives in a particular pattern that is a useful model to copy to make your own writing more interesting:

> The <u>quieter</u> I became at school the <u>louder</u> my mother became at home.

• Complete the sentences below by adding a second comparative adjective.

The darker it became … *the less they could see.*
The longer the holiday …
The harder I worked …
The easier the test …
The more they argued …
The sooner we leave …

• Now write five examples of your own using the same pattern.

Vocabulary | You will need SB pp170–171 & pp174–176 |

- Write your own interpretation of the following phrases from the poem 'The Roc' (pages 170–171 of your Student Book) to show that you understand their meanings.

time in mosque sounds	calls to prayer at the mosque indicating different parts of the day
chinking them awake	
seized them up	
alien phonemes	
the little budget	
friendly natives	
the newly landed	

- Find the verbs or phrasal verbs to match these meanings in 'Coming home' on pages 174–176 in your Student Book. Line numbers are provided to help you find the synonyms in the extract.

arrives (line 6)	pulls into	consider (line 34)	
mix and move (line 7)		twisting (line 43)	
enjoying (line 9)		getting close (line 45)	
disappears (line 16)		stretching (line 53)	
vibrant (line 22)		amazed (line 58)	
inspired (line 31)		know (line 60)	
churning (line 32)		fixed (line 61)	

Extension Write sentences of your own using five of the verbs you found in 'Coming home' to show how they can be used to express different experiences.

Writing from the second-person point of view

> You will need SB pp163–169 & pp174–176

Point of view is the narrative voice you choose to write in. It can be first person ('I', 'my'), second person ('you', 'your') or third person ('he'/'she'/'they' and 'his'/'hers'/'theirs').

Look carefully at the second-person point of view in 'Coming home'. This is a less common perspective for writers to use, and here it helps to add to the intensity of the experience through its direct address to the reader.

- Choose a paragraph from another text in the Student Book, such as 'Becoming too American' or 'Learning the English', and rewrite it in the second person.

Extension Analyze your version of the text from the activity above, as if you are writing a critical review. What is striking about it?

Writing about a place

- Write a short text in poetry or prose form about the experience of leaving somewhere you have enjoyed. It could be a holiday or day trip, or leaving a place you used to live. Try to include analogy or metaphor, and other literary devices to structure and enhance your writing.

12 Fashion conscious

In this unit, you will practise using hyphenated compound phrases, *up-* and *down-*words and descriptive language, write a statement about being fashion conscious and a description of a fashionista, and design a promotional poster.

Writing a statement

Even if you don't care about fashion, you still make fashion choices (or they are made for you). Think about how you dress and present yourself to the world. Do you think about how your clothes are made, what they are made of and where they come from?

- Write your own statement here about what you think it means to be 'fashion conscious'.

Extension Read the statement you wrote above. Which aspect of being 'fashion conscious' is most important to you?

Compound phrases that use hyphens

Hyphens are the small dashes that join words together to make compound phrases easier to understand. For this reason, they are useful in writing extended descriptions of a noun, as in the examples:

'record-breaking snow'

'lime-green leggings'

- Insert hyphens in the correct places in the sentences below. The first one has been done for you.

The apple-green sari was a gift from her aunts.	We donated much needed winter clothing to them.
She wore candy striped glass bangles.	He wore army style fatigues as a fashion choice.
He is a self employed fashion designer.	What's that moth eaten cardigan you are wearing?
They had created a plastic free clothing line.	She wore a hot pink T shirt to stand out in the crowd.
The ill fitting garment was not comfortable to wear.	His old jeans had that fashionable distressed denim look.

- Now write five sentences of your own on fashion choices that use hyphenated compound phrases.

Extension Find other examples of hyphenated compound phrases in the extracts in this unit or a novel you are currently reading.

Words with the prefix *up-*

Up- words are often used to show progress, positive change or ascendence (going higher).

● Complete each sentence below with an *up-* word from the following list:

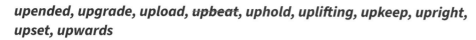

upended, upgrade, upload, ~~upbeat~~, uphold, uplifting, upkeep, upright, upset, upwards

People are always attracted to her positive, _____ upbeat _____ personality.

His gaze was fixed _____ to the squirrel at the top of the tree.

He returned the vase to its _____ position and noticed the crack.

We will _____ the computer software when the office is closed.

We'd like a big garden, but they do require a lot of _____.

It was an _____ experience for the entire school community.

Before her mother could stop him, the toddler _____ the bowl.

The twins were _____ when they were put in separate classes.

The judge ruled to _____ the conviction with a reduced sentence.

I need to _____ my photos to the online picture library.

● Now write five sentences of your own, including an *up-* word in each one. You can use the *up-* words above and/or think of other ones.

Words with the prefix *down-*

Down- words are used to describe something lower in position, amount or quality. This isn't always a bad thing!

- Complete each sentence below with a *down-* word from the following list:

  downgrade, downhearted, download, downplay, downpour, downstream, downtime, downsize, downstairs, downwind

---

They all needed some _____downtime_____ now that the exams were over.

Luckily, the hurricane got a _____ to a tropical storm warning.

There is much more erosion on the _____ side of the beach.

"Meet me _____ and we'll sneak out the back way," she said.

It is easier to travel _____ than against the river current.

Many older couples _____ when their children leave home.

A _____ of rain put out the bonfire and they ran for shelter.

Irresponsible companies often _____ the environmental risks.

The _____ from the internet took longer than she expected.

They were _____ for weeks after the festival was cancelled.

- Now write five sentences of your own, including a *down-* word in each one. You can use the *down-* words above and/or think of other ones.

Promote a new fashion store

- In preparation for designing a promotional poster or billboard for the opening of a new fashion store or clothes shop, note down the essential information to include in the table below.

Name of the store	
Location	
Date of opening	
Special offers	
Target customers	

- Sketch out your poster in the space below. You might like to include graphics, colour and different font sizes to make your poster stand out and to highlight particular information.

Descriptive language | You will need SB pp191–192

- Reread the text 'Paris Fashion Week' and find the words or phrases which mean the following (line numbers are provided to help you):

renew interest (line 14)	reinspire	order (line 37)	
looked with great surprise (line 26)		to beat (line 42)	
falling like water (line 28)		understanding (line 49)	
valuable (line 30)		work together (line 52)	
covered in gems (line 34)		angrily (line 58)	

Writing a description

- Write a paragraph describing someone you know, or a celebrity, who behaves like a fashionista and what you like or dislike about their love of fashion.

Extension Write three to four sentences of your own using some of the words and phrases from the activity at the top of this page.

Cross-curricular words to help you at school

Here are all the cross-curricular words you are learning this year. Highlight any words you don't know and read the definitions. Use this list for reference as you complete the activities on the following pages.

advise *verb* to give somebody advice; to inform somebody about something
  'I can advise you on what to take on the school trip.'

alien *noun* in stories, a being from another world; a foreigner
  'During the war, he was imprisoned as an enemy alien.'
  adjective foreign; unnatural or unfamiliar
  'When I first went overseas, it felt very alien to me.'

analysis *noun* a detailed examination of something
  'The book is an analysis of climate change.'

assert *verb* to state something firmly
  'She continued to assert her innocence.'

compatible *adjective* able to live or exist together without trouble
  'The business partners stopped working together because their values were not compatible.'

conceal *verb* to hide someone or something, or keep them secret
  'She was unable to conceal her disappointment in her test result.'

condemn *verb* to say that you strongly disapprove of something
  'Most people condemn cruelty to animals.'

conform *verb* to keep to accepted rules, customs or ideas
  'All students must conform to the rules of the school.'

confront *verb* to face up to and deal with a problem; to challenge someone face to face
  'She knew she had to confront her fear of heights to climb to the top of the building.'

consensus *noun* general agreement; the opinion of most people
  'The consensus is that global temperatures will get warmer.'

conventional *adjective* done or doing things in the normal or accepted way; traditional
  'She gives the impression of being very conventional.'

conviction *noun* the process of convicting someone of a crime; firm opinion or belief
  'He said he agreed but his voice lacked conviction.'

customary *adjective* in accordance with custom; usual
  'It is customary to say congratulations when people have good news.'

deduce *verb* to work something out by reasoning from facts that you know are true
  'The police were able to deduce where the fugitive was hiding.'

dilemma *noun* a situation where someone has to choose between two or more possible actions, either of which would bring difficulties
  'She faced a dilemma about whether to accept the job offer or go travelling.'

distress *noun* great sorrow, pain, or trouble
  'A lifeboat was sent out to a ship in distress.'

equality *noun* the state of being equal
  'Do you believe in equality between men and women?'

evoke *verb* to produce or inspire a memory or feelings
'The photographs evoke memories of my childhood.'

harmony *noun* friendly and peaceful feelings between people
'There was perfect harmony between the two brothers.'

hypothetical *adjective* based on a theory or possibility; supposed but not necessarily real or true
'Let's look at a hypothetical situation where you get invited to two parties.'

imply *verb* to suggest something without actually saying it
'The girl had not meant to imply that he was lying.'

infer *verb* to work something out from what someone says or does
'I can infer that you are going to say yes.'

innovation *noun* a completely new process or way of doing things that has just been introduced
'The company is very interested in product design and innovation.'

intense *adjective* very strong or great
'He struggled to finish the race in the intense heat.'

justify *verb* to show that something is fair, just or reasonable
'How can you justify spending so much money?'

moral *noun* a lesson in right and wrong behaviour taught by a story or event
'The moral of this story is that crime doesn't pay.'

adjective connected with what is right and wrong in behaviour
'We have a moral obligation to protect the environment.'

obtain *verb* to get or be given something
'You can obtain a copy of the book here.'

opposition *noun* the action of opposing something; resistance
'The army met with fierce opposition in every town.'

pacify *verb* to calm a person down
'It was difficult for the police to pacify the angry crowd.'

prevalent *adjective* most frequent or common; widespread
'Trees are dying in areas where acid rain is most prevalent.'

prove *verb* to show that something is true
'Can you prove that what you say is true?'

represent *verb* to do something on someone's behalf; to be an example of something
'The poet used the metaphor of fire to represent hatred.'

sensible *adjective* wise; having or showing good sense
'It was sensible of you to lock the door before going out.'

structure *noun* something that has been constructed or built
'The teacher asked us to draw a diagram of the structure of a leaf.'

verb to organize or arrange something into a system or pattern
'How well does your teacher structure the lessons?'

subconscious *adjective* to do with mental processes of which we are not fully aware but which influence our actions
'Was someone behind him, or was his subconscious mind taking over?'

noun the part of the mind in which these processes take place
'Early childhood experiences can create fears in the subconscious.'

universal *adjective* to do with, including or done by everyone or everything
'The dove is a universal symbol of peace.'

vindicate *verb* to clear a person of blame or suspicion
'The investigation vindicated her complaint about the newspaper.'

widespread *adjective* existing in many places or over a wide area
'The hurricane caused widespread damage and disruption.'

Practice

1 Match the underlined word in each sentence to the word with the same meaning.

Is it possible to <u>show</u> beyond doubt that dinosaurs once lived on this planet?	conform
He felt an <u>extreme</u> pain in his back.	prove
He made a half-hearted attempt to <u>explain</u> his behaviour.	justify
Students will be punished if they do not <u>stick</u> to the school rules.	harmony
My parents hardly ever argue – I really admire the <u>peace</u> in their relationship.	intense

2 Fill in the missing words in each sentence with one of the words below.

evoke, conceal, pacify, dilemma, opposition, analysis

   a The mother tried to _____ her crying baby by singing nursery rhymes.

   b There is strong _____ to the latest plans to build more houses in our town.

   c Smells and tastes often _____ memories from the past.

   d When I saw my friend cheating in the test, I faced a real _____ – should I tell the teacher or not?

   e He tried to _____ his yawn behind his hand.

   f Our homework was to write an _____ of how we spend our free time.

3 Write sentences of your own for each of the words below.

imply, confront, conviction, condemn, structure

   a _____

   b _____

   c _____

   d _____

   e _____

4 Find a synonym (a word with the same meaning) and an antonym (a word with the opposite meaning) for each of the words in the grid and add them to the appropriate column.

	Synonym	Antonym
customary	routine	irregular
obtain		
sensible		
distress		
prevalent		
vindicate		

5 How many new words can you make from these words? You can add or remove letters, find words within words, rearrange letters, and add prefixes or suffixes. Then write sentences using the new words.

represent	
innovation	
universal	
deduce	
hypothetical	
widespread	

6 Fill in the speech bubbles using one of the words from the box in each bubble. You can change the form of the word to make it fit, for example, "I will work out what happened yesterday at lunchtime by logical <u>deduction</u>!" You can make the bubbles as funny or unusual as you like. Work with a partner and use your imagination. Use a dictionary or the internet to help with spelling.

deduce   **conventional**   **equality**   **subconscious**

7 Now it's time to get really creative!

If you are working with a partner:

- Choose and write down **six** words from the list on pages 83–85 that you think are the most useful.
- Take turns to explain a word to your partner without looking at the definitions on pages 83–85 and WITHOUT SAYING THE WORD.

If you are working alone:

- Choose and write down **six** words from the list on pages 83–85 that you think are the most useful.
- Write a short story that includes the **six** words. You can add prefixes and suffixes to the words as well.
- You might like to refer to the images below to give you inspiration for your story.

8 You are going to write a news report on a subject of your choice. In the report, you must include at least **six** cross-curricular words from pages 83–85. You can either write them in the box below before you begin, or decide on the words as you write and then add them to the box.

-
-
-

-
-
-

Grammar and language terms

action tag short description of a character's action(s) during a dialogue exchange to indicate who is speaking and perhaps how they are feeling; provides alternative to a dialogue tag such as 'she said'

"I'm sorry." <u>She hung her head and shuffled in embarrassment</u>.

active voice a set of verb forms in which the subject of a verb performs the action. Compare with **passive voice**.

'The dog is chasing the cat.'

adverbial a word or phrase which gives more information about a verb or about a clause. An adverbial can be an adverb, a phrase or a subordinate clause.

Adverbials tell you where, when, why, how or how often something was done.
'The dog slept <u>under</u> the table.'
'I <u>usually</u> do my homework before I watch TV.'
'Jack worked <u>very hard</u>.'
'The cat sleeps <u>all day</u>.'

Adverbials sometimes appear at the beginning of a sentence. These are called 'fronted adverbials'. There is usually a comma after a fronted adverbial.
'<u>First thing in the morning</u>, I walk the dog.'
'<u>Next</u>, I have my breakfast.'

Some adverbials link ideas across paragraphs or within paragraphs. These adverbials are often fronted and are usually followed by a comma.
'on the other hand'; 'in contrast'; 'as a result'; 'secondly'

adverbs of frequency describe how often something happens. They include 'always', 'usually', 'often', 'sometimes', 'rarely', and 'never'.
'We <u>usually</u> have sandwiches for lunch.'

alliteration occurs when two or more nearby words start with the same sound
'A <u>s</u>low, <u>s</u>ad, <u>s</u>orrowful <u>s</u>ong.'

anthropomorphism giving human characteristics, emotions or behaviours to animals, things and gods. Characters like Simba and the other talking lions from *The Lion King*, the Cheshire Cat, the Caterpillar and the White Rabbit from *Alice in Wonderland*, and the gods from Greek mythology are examples of anthropomorphism.

attributive adjective an adjective that comes before the word it describes. Compare with **predicative adjective**.
'a <u>diligent</u> student'

auxiliary verbs these are used with main verbs to indicate continuous actions or to form different tenses. 'Be' and 'have' are auxiliary verbs.
'I <u>am</u> eating.'
'It <u>has</u> rained all night.'

The auxiliary verb 'do' is used in negative statements, questions and commands.
'I <u>do not</u> want any more chocolate.'
'<u>Do</u> you want some?'
'<u>Do</u> sit still!'

circumstance adverbs consist of three main types of adverbs: manner (for example, 'happily'), time (for example, 'after') and place (for example, 'at school')

clause a group of words that contains a subject and a verb. Every full sentence contains at least one main clause.
'I ran.' (In this clause, 'I' is the subject and 'ran' is the verb.)

Multi-clause sentences contain one or more subordinate clauses. A subordinate clause does not make sense on its own and relies on the main clause.
'When I had finished reading it, I returned the book to the library.' (In this sentence, the clause 'When I had finished reading it' is a subordinate clause, which depends on the main clause, 'I returned the book to the library' to make sense.)

colloquial language suitable for conversation but not for formal speech or writing

comparative comparative adjectives are used when two things are being compared
'Morning break is only fifteen minutes, but the lunch break is longer.'

complex sentence a sentence with one independent clause and at least one dependent clause (a clause that does not make sense on its own)
'Because it was raining, they decided to take the bus.'

compound sentence a compound sentence is made up of two independent clauses (clauses that make sense on their own). These are connected by a coordinating conjunction, such as 'for', 'and', 'nor', 'but', 'or', 'yet' or 'so'.
'She likes swimming, but she doesn't like running.'

conditional (relating to) a sentence that expresses that one thing is dependent on something else. Conditional sentences often begin with 'If ...' or 'Unless ...'.
'If I win this race, I will get a prize.'

conjunctive adverb a type of adverb that joins two clauses in a sentence, creating a link between them. Conjunctive adverbs can also show the cause and effect of an action.
'accordingly'; 'also'; 'besides'; 'consequently'; 'finally'; 'however'; 'indeed'; 'instead'

contraction when an apostrophe is used to show that letters have been removed from a word
'didn't' (for 'did not'); 'it's' (for 'it is')

dash clause an independent clause connected to another by a dash. The second clause is often introduced by a conjunction such as 'and', 'as', 'but', 'for', 'or', 'yet'. The dash works like commas but has more impact. It is less formal than a colon or brackets.
'He quickly ate his lunch – he was always in a hurry.'
'I want my lunch – and I want it now!'

determiner a word like 'a', 'the', 'some', 'any', 'my', 'each', 'every', 'either' and 'no' which is used before a noun, or at the start of a noun phrase. Determiners tell you which one, how many or how much.
'The girls enjoyed the music.'
'There is a bird on the branch.'
'Each box contained 20 books.'

direct speech when speech marks are used to show that someone is speaking
"Can I talk to you, please?" asked Sam.

expanded noun phrases a noun phrase has a noun as its head, or key word: 'ball' (noun); 'the ball' (noun phrase). Expanded noun phrases add more detail to the noun by adding one or more adjectives, or by saying where the noun is.
'the red pencil on the floor by the desk'

figurative language uses words for the effects they create, rather than their literal meanings. It often produces vivid images and sounds in the mind of the reader or listener. The most common types of figurative language are: simile, metaphor, personification, hyperbole and onomatopoeia.
'This homework will take forever!' (hyperbole)
'My hands are as cold as ice.' (simile)
'Her eyes blazed with anger.' (metaphor)

genre a type of writing. Poetry, fantasy and non-fiction are examples of different genres.

gerund a form of a verb that ends in -*ing* and that is used as a noun
'Many teenagers enjoy <u>playing</u> video games.'

homographs words that are spelled the same way but not necessarily pronounced the same way and have different meanings and origins
Spelled the same way but pronounced differently:
'A <u>tear</u> rolled down Sasha's cheek.'
'<u>Tear</u> the form off and send it to the address below.'
Spelled and pronounced the same way:
'The head teacher <u>rose</u> from her seat.'
'The ball landed in the <u>rose</u> bushes.'

homophones one of two or more words that sound the same but have different meanings. They may have the same or different spellings.
'right' and 'write'; 'meat' and 'meet'

idiom an expression that cannot be understood from the literal meanings of its separate words. It has a figurative meaning that needs to be understood as a whole.
'It's raining cats and dogs.' (This means that it is raining very hard.)

imperative the form of the verb used to make commands
'<u>Go</u> away!'

indirect speech another name for **reported speech**

infinitive the form of a verb that does not change to indicate a particular tense or number or person, in English used with or without 'to'
'go': 'I will go', 'Let me go' or 'Allow me to go'

irregular verb any verb that does not follow the expected pattern of conjugation in some way. In English, this is usually by not adding -*ed* or -*d* to its past tense form.
'go' (went), 'is' (was), 'do' (did), 'eat' (ate), 'get' (got), 'have' (had), 'make' (made)

main verb the most important verb in the sentence. It describes the action or state of the subject of the sentence.
'The children <u>climbed</u> the tree.'
'We <u>ate</u> a large bar of chocolate during the film.'

metaphor a way of speaking or writing in which one thing is said to be something else. This way of speaking or writing is called a figure of speech.
'Thanks for your help – <u>you are a star</u>!'

modal verb used with a verb to show what is possible, necessary, or what is going to happen
'I <u>should</u> go for a walk.'

multi-clause sentence a sentence that consists of more than one clause

noun phrase a small group of words containing a noun or pronoun and one or more modifiers
'My new blue jacket.'

passive voice verb forms in which the subject of the sentence is the person or thing affected by the verb. It is formed using the **auxiliary verb** 'be' and the **past participle**. Compare with **active voice**.
'A window <u>was broken</u>.'

past participle formed from a verb (usually by adding -d or -ed to the root form, for example 'guide' becomes 'guided'). It is generally used with an auxiliary verb ('has', 'have' or 'had') to construct the perfect tenses.
'She <u>has gone</u> to school.'

Past participles can be used as adjectives.
'<u>burnt</u> toast'; 'a <u>broken</u> pencil'

perfect tense verb tense used to refer to an action that is already completed at the time of speaking about it
'He <u>has tidied</u> his bedroom.'
'They <u>had spoken</u> about their concerns.'

personification the technique of giving human qualities to things that are not human, such as an animal, a concept or an inanimate object
'The <u>sun beamed happily</u> while the <u>kittens played hide-and-seek</u>, and <u>life danced by</u>.'

phrasal verb an expression using a verb combined with a preposition and/or an adverb. In a phrasal verb, the individual words often do not have their usual meaning.
'Please <u>look after</u> your little brother.'
'He <u>went off</u> down the road.'

phrase a small group of words that forms part of a clause. Phrases do not make sense on their own.

possessive pronouns these are used instead of the noun to show who or what something belongs to. They are: 'mine', 'yours', 'his', 'hers', 'ours' and 'theirs'.
'Is that school jumper <u>mine</u> or <u>yours</u>?'

Possessive adjectives are used with nouns to show who or what it belongs to or is related to: 'my', 'your', 'his', 'her', 'its', 'our' and 'their'.
'That is <u>my</u> school jumper.'

Possessive forms of a name or noun have **'s** added to them.
'<u>Aalina's</u> books'
'the <u>children's</u> shoes'
'The politicians' manifestos' (note: with a plural ending in 's', the apostrophe comes after the 's')

predicative adjective an adjective that comes after a linking verb such as 'be' or 'seem' and forms part of the predicate. Compare with **attributive adjective**.
'The student is <u>diligent</u>.'

prefix a word or syllable placed at the beginning of a word to modify its meaning. In the word 'misunderstand', the prefix *mis-* makes the word 'understand' mean 'not understand correctly'. In the word 'unhappy', the prefix *un-* makes the word 'happy' mean 'not happy'.

preposition a word that indicates place ('on', 'in'), direction ('over', 'beyond') or time ('during', 'on') among others
'I read my book <u>during</u> lunch. I put the book <u>in</u> the drawer.'

present participle this is usually formed by adding *-ing* to the infinitive of the verb. They are sometimes used as adjectives and sometimes as nouns.
'We have been <u>working</u> hard all day.'
'<u>Swimming</u> is a popular sport.'

relative clause a type of subordinate clause introduced using relative pronouns such as 'that', 'which', 'who', 'whom', and 'whose'
'Whales are mammals <u>that live in the sea</u>.'

reported speech when you report someone's words in a changed form
"I am at home." (direct speech)
'She said she was at home.' (reported speech)

simile a figure of speech in which two things are compared using the linking words 'like' or 'as'
'She was <u>as quick as lightning</u>.'

simple present tense used when an action is happening at the present moment, or when it happens regularly
'He <u>gets</u> up very early every morning.'

subordinate clause a clause which adds details to the main clause of the sentence but cannot be used as a sentence by itself
'<u>When I finish my homework</u>, I will go and meet my friends.'

suffix a word or syllable placed at the end of a word to modify its meaning. In the word 'tasteless', the suffix *-less* makes the word 'tasteless' mean 'with no taste'.

superlative superlative adjectives and adverbs are used to compare and contrast three or more people, things or actions. The superlative shows which is greatest or most and is generally formed by adding *-est* or *-st*.
'Cheetahs are the <u>fastest</u> land animals.'

synonym a word or phrase that means exactly or nearly the same as another word or phrase in the same language
For example, the verb 'shut' is a synonym of the verb 'close'.

third conditional the third conditional is used to talk about a situation in the past that did **not** happen. Sentences have an 'if' part and a main/result part. The third conditional consists of 'if' + *past perfect* and 'would have' + *past participle*.
'If I had realized you didn't like chocolate cake, I would have brought something else.'

verb phrase a group of words, including the main verb and any other linking verbs or modifiers, that act as a sentence's verb
'My brother <u>is studying</u> in his room.'